SHADOWS OF THE SOUL

Edited by

Heather Killingray

First published in Great Britain in 1999 by
POETRY NOW
Remus House,
Coltsfoot Drive,
Woodston,
Peterborough, PE2 9JX
Telephone (01733) 898101
Fax (01733) 313524

All Rights Reserved

Copyright Contributors 1999

HB ISBN 0 75430 731 X
SB ISBN 0 75430 732 8

FOREWORD

Although we are a nation of poetry writers we are accused of not reading poetry and not buying poetry books: after many years of listening to the incessant gripes of poetry publishers, I can only assume that the books they publish, in general, are books that most people do not want to read.
Poetry should not be obscure, introverted, and as cryptic as a crossword puzzle: it is the poet's duty to reach out and embrace the world.
The world owes the poet nothing and we should not be expected to dig and delve into a rambling discourse searching for some inner meaning.
The reason we write poetry (and almost all of us do) is because we want to communicate: an ideal; an idea; or a specific feeling. Poetry is as essential in communication, as a letter; a radio; a telephone, and the main criteria for selecting the poems in this anthology is very simple: they communicate.

CONTENTS

Night Whispers	Shirley Williamson	1
Night Terrors	Rita Furnival	2
Some Intruder	Jean Rendell	3
For Someone Walking Conjures Up Stalking	John P Evans	4
Guided Through Dark Night	James Leonard Clough	5
Night Whispers	Judith E Bradley	6
The Language Of Silence	Marion Payton	7
A Starless Night's Walk	Alma Montgomery Frank	8
Night-Time Comes And Night-Time Goes	Keith L Powell	9
Lighten Our Darkness	Paddy Jupp	10
Piccadilly Gardens	Marion Hadfield	11
Forbidden Night	Ann Hathaway	12
The Nocturnal Fae	Bernadette Morris	13
Night Whispers	Margaret Jackson	14
Highland Nights	Alister H Thomson	15
Night Whispers	Ann Voaden	16
Facing Fax	Betty Lightfoot	17
Eternal Nights	P Sharp	18
Night Whispers	Janet A Rimmer	19
The Haunted House	Penni Nicolson	20
Mother Nature	J M Stoles	21
Night Into Day	June Ingoldby Holmes	22
The Train Ran Over A Human Sleeper	Gillian C Fisher	23
My Experience	Cindy White	24
The Last Chance	Colin Mackay	25
One Last Chance	Phyllis O'Connell	26
Life Will Find A Way	Michaela W Garlick	27
One Last Chance	Annemarie Poole	28
The Final Day	June Plange	29
Our Future	Richard Reeve	30
Uncertain Planet	Nevin McCloy	31
Life Moves So Fast	Naomi Elisa Price	32
The Wandering Path	John Amsden	33

Realism	Barbara Beaumont	34
The Pirate Of The Holy Grail	David de Pinna	35
Domino Effect	Robert Thompson	36
Is The World Going To Come To A Standstill?	Jean Rickwood	37
Night Whispers	B Bowles	38
My Last Night	Janet Cavill	39
24 Hours	Gail Walker	40
A Ticket To Mars	Roger Williams	41
Darkness Of Night	Doreen A Swann	42
When I Was Young	Ivy Neville	43
Afternoon Tea	Rosalie Wells	44
To A Long-Lost Friend	Julia Eva Yeardye	45
The Way Of Life	Ann Dutschak	46
Passing Of A Friend	T G Bloodworth	47
He Loves Me Really	Linda Woodhouse	48
Toties Two Years On	H G Griffiths	49
The Washing Cycle	Karen Hollinghurst	50
He's Won The Cup!	John L Wright & 'Jackdaw'	51
A Stranger Within	Siobhan Cleary	52
Another Week	Kenneth Mood	53
Time	Angela Pritchard	54
My Cab Driver	Alan Cornelius	55
Back To School	Tanya McCollum	56
Each Chiefly	Rio	57
The Garden Of Echoes	E F Parker	58
The Dales	Tom Ritchie	59
Shepherd's Delight	Betty Mealand	60
I'll Still Love You	K Lake	61
Clocking Out	J Wren	62
What Was That Dream?	Colin Allsop	63
Without You	P Allen	64
We Decide	Alice Michell	65
A World For The Future	Georgina Forrest	66
Environment	Jonathon Simons	67
A World For The Future?	Tambi Maple	68
The Future?	Simon Barlow	69
After The Storm	Kimberly Harries	70

Philosophy	Martin Buckley	71
If I Won The Lottery	Jill Johnson	72
Poem About Maureen	D McDonald	73
The Juice Of Nature!	Natalie Iley	74
The Rose	Heather Rowley	75
Baby Blues	Frank Howarth-Hynes	76
Goodbye	Sahdia-Sarah Suraiyya	77
Music Is In The Air	Heather Aspinall	78
Passing Time	R P Scannell	79
My Thoughts Of Boys	Kayleigh Rosewarne	80
Boys	Nicola Jane Strapp-Freeman	81
Boys	Emma Rigden	82
Take Boys	Felicity Anne Carter	83
The Boy	Natasha Clarke	84
Girls On Boys	Catherine Manderson	85
Girls On Boys	Mary Poynter	86
Untitled	Anne-Marie Toth	87
A World For The Future Good/Bad	Amy Frances White	88
Pig Rabbit Ear	Sally McLardy	89
Consumatum Est	J Baker	90
The Journey	Joan Wylde	91
Night Wind	Florence Andrews	92
170-Odd Candles On The Cake?	Joyce Hockley	93
The Burglar	Andrew Mackie	94
Wanton Love	Pam Gibbons	95
Being Disabled	Trisha Moreton	96
Life's Misfortune	Mansel	97
A True Friendship	Joan A Anscombe	98
Boys (From A Girl's Point Of View)	Kathryn McCandless	99
Girls Differ From Boys	Fateha Begum	100
It's Not Too Late	Sandy Grebby	101
Coming Of Age	Margaret Parnell	102
Andrea Jennet (1986)	Jan Lingard	103
The Pause Of Peace	Tay Collicutt	104
Shadows Calling	Dragon	105
Alun Armstrong!	Kimberley M Rushforth	106

A World For The Future . . .	Kerrie Nightingale	107
Your Arms About Me	Joan E Blissett	108
Fields Of Adventure	Wendy Watkin	109
Autumn	Dan Pugh	110

NIGHT WHISPERS

As shadows, growing longer
Bring evening into night,
Silent wings take off now
To make a homeward flight.

The tinge of sun, now setting
Forms silhouettes against the sky,
Soon fading to oblivion
As the moon alights on high.

Shadows all melt into one
To form the dark night sky,
Nocturnal life now wakens
To fly or scurry by.

An aura of well-being,
As quiet peace surrounds,
Gives off a mellow feeling
As the day's life settles down.

The cloak of night brings comfort
From the ever-bustling day,
Massaging all the troubles
From the shoulders of the world.

Shirley Williamson

NIGHT TERRORS

Where does the dark go, Mummy
when you switch on my bedside light?
Does it hide at the back of the cupboard
waiting to give me a fright?

Where does the night go, Mummy
when the sun peeps over the hill?
Does it run to the shelter of Big Wood
and of dampness and cold drink its fill?

Where does the wind go, Mummy
when it's chased all the green leaves away
and it howls like a beast in the chimney -
it might break loose in the day!

Where did my dad go, Mummy
when you yelled at each other all night?
Is he really in hell where you wished him -
and please can you leave on the light?

Rita Furnival

SOME INTRUDER

Midnight the clock strikes in the hall
Awakened to a noise, was that a fall?
The door lock's stuck the panel breaks
Call 999 emergency life's at stake.
Lying petrified under the covers,
Footsteps on the stairs, please don't me they discover.
Closer now fear grips my heart
Heavy breathing oh why did he start?
Cupboard doors opened clothes tossed aside
Seeking through my things, this I can't abide.
Reach for my bag handle grasped ready
Covers back silent and deadly.
Aim for the head, wham a goal in one
Now the fun's really begun.
Light switched on drunken husband's lying on the floor
That will teach him to break down our door.

Jean Rendell

FOR SOMEONE WALKING CONJURES UP STALKING?

When you walk alone from work each night, you walk home via
                                                                       the park,
You hear phantom footsteps, in the silence of the dark.
A fallacious human thought, it has you stealthily walking away,
For some people the night conjures up images in mind, but is there a better way?

John P Evans

GUIDED THROUGH DARK NIGHT

Nineteenth century drovers,
With four hundred Welsh cattle;
Faced cold, mist and dark marshes,
Bala to Sussex Battle.
Fifteen long hours to nightfall,
For three weeks winter's snow squall.

Limping noisy cavalcade,
Of black cows, sheep, pigs and dogs;
Faced bloodthirsty brigands' raid,
In cloudy overcast fogs.
Drovers' money in waistbands,
Easy dupes for cut-throat bands.

Drovers planned expedition,
Placed lights by treacherous bog.
Hid in rocky position,
Hailed robbers with barking dog.
Rustlers plunged to nameless death,
Rangers rallied with quick breath.

Screeching night owls' haunting cry,
Made farmers link arms in scorn
Of bandits who scarify
And steal runts, ponies, longhorn.
Rebellious rogues now subdued,
Despair quenched by fortitude.

Surrounded by danger's foes,
Single against darkest night.
With armour of faith, oppose,
Stand firm in immortal might.
Rock of Ages sure defence,
Triumph watchful providence.

James Leonard Clough

NIGHT WHISPERS

Every day I walk home this way
Past the fields, and hedges high
Sun is shining, with a gentle breeze
Swaying arms of old oak trees
Rabbits peeping in and out of holes
Dark earth mounds made by moles
Birds are singing out their song
I don't mind that the lane is long.

But if I'm late in coming back
And night has come, I start down the track
Everything has changed, in my torch-light
Each rustle I hear gives me a fright
What is that shape down in the ditch
That oak tree looks just like a witch
What is that scream, vixen or crying child
Now my imagination is running wild.

I break into a run for home right now
Sweat is dropping from my brow
Heart is thumping, pain is strong
Oh my God, this lane is long
But there's a light shining, can you see
Soon be home, he's looking out for me
With kisses, hugs and a cup of tea
And I'm thinking, silly me.

Judith E Bradley

THE LANGUAGE OF SILENCE

In the language of silence,
When day turns to night,
There's a creaking, a squeaking,
A speaking that might
Be the door or the floor
Or the cat with his paws
Strolling the tiles -
That's what rooftops are for!
Then the moonlight casts shadows
Creeping along, to the song
Of the owl and the bat
Oh, how long before
Sleep brings its dreams?
Then a voice clearly seems
To say, 'Don't be fearful,
I am here;' night time scenes
Can't darken the light
Of my language that means
Peace and protection.
So listen and hear -
My love is the watchman
That guards you from fear.

Marion Payton

A STARLESS NIGHT'S WALK

My walk was on a night that was cold
Icy fingers seemed to touch
My face and leave patches
Of light I knew that brightened the night
Some tiny creature passed over my foot
I trembled at the thought
But walked on the faster
Something fluttered into my hair
A bat no doubt but I hardly dare
To make the discovery
But it flew away in an instance
Though it seemed a lifetime
All of a sudden I heard the hoot of an owl
It seemed to warn me of a fast coming intrusion
In the distance four blazing lights
A swish! A horn! One almost
Stumbled, missed by a whisker
Gone! The near flying owl
Hoots again, goodbye you interfering
Monster! How wonderful the lane
The new solitude, the sky with
Its tender light at last, could it be
The moon, no it's too dark!
All once more settles down to a night
Perhaps full of heavenly bliss
Especially me as I walk
With merry steps towards
My home in the village
What a real treat, I have not been molested!
One has to be thankful
These crime ridden days.

Alma Montgomery Frank

NIGHT-TIME COMES AND NIGHT-TIME GOES

Night-time comes and night-time goes
With so many things I just say oh
For in the daylight I do all I can
As when the night arrives I see a frightened woman.

Night-time comes and night-time goes
It will always be the same this I know
Yet I feel so alone
Yet in the daylight I feel so happy and content.

Night-time comes and night-time goes
Yet everybody says I will be all right
That with the dark I can cure my fright
For there are others just like me
Who have got over it.

Keith L Powell

LIGHTEN OUR DARKNESS

When will electric power be found and put back on again?
We've been 'off' now since Friday and it's Sunday morn' - so when?
Has it vanished then forever and if so where's it gone?
We're missing it in our road - it's still 'off' it's sure not 'on'!
It left in such a hurry, blown away in one blue flash,
Crazily zigzagging out and cutting quite a dash.
It hasn't reappeared yet and so cannot be reused
To boost our flagging spirits, not to mention plugs refused.
We're told maybe tomorrow or the next day, but no luck,
The people who we speak to just don't know, or pass the buck.
The candlelight's now palling, cooking meals by torch-light's grim,
Our houses are all freezing and our patience growing thin.
Now it's nearly Monday, four days gone without some power,
Requesting news again we're told 'Can't tell you any hour.'
So we're just left to wait until we see the van appear
And men with grins say 'You're back on my loves' then disappear!

Paddy Jupp

Piccadilly Gardens

Piccadilly gardens are so bright,
On a lovely summer night.
Blossom trees fill the air,
People sit just anywhere.
Flowers look up to the sky,
Lots of people walk on by.
Darkness comes - people go,
Look in there faces - 'Does it show'
That they have, nowhere to go?
They live on the streets,
Just a cover to show.
Is it there fault - do we want to know?

Marion Hadfield

FORBIDDEN NIGHT

Loneliness brings twilight creeping
Shadowy figures around me sneaking
Every sound trembles my bones
Who walks there on dark drive stones
Close eyes shut out ghostly shape
Duvet surrounds 'tis my comfort cape
Restless fluttering throbbing towards sleep
Edge me sweet dreams towards total abyss
Surrounded by angels then grant forever wish
Don't let me die before waking from slumber
Still beating hearts overwhelming thunder
Eerie shades across window I see
Beautiful face young girl who once was me
Black reaper stalks he comes knocking
Fearful nightmares evil faces mocking
Nightmares lonely stilled hours immensely endless
Visions from forever weigh tremendous
Morning bring your inviting light
So fearful am I about the night

Ann Hathaway

The Nocturnal Fae

The dark nocturnal faerie is handsome to behold
Yet sightings are unlikely because he's far from bold.
He's smaller than a human, yet muscularly compact
His strength is unbelievable, if he should choose to act.

His skin is smooth and creamy pale, his eyes are black as night
And sometimes these can flare with flame to burn you out of sight.
His raven hair is shot throughout with red or green or blue
And sometimes even violet of an iridescent hue.

His wings are black and leathery, just like those of a bat
They span his height and twice again. One beat could knock you flat.
And yet he doesn't often need these pinions to unfold
For he can teleport at will to places yet untold.

His teeth are very white and sharp, his canines elongated
But he won't bite just anyone; he wants you to be mated.
He'll sip your blood with relish, if you are on his level
But if you're not he'll pass you by, he doesn't need a devil.

If you are not 'suitable', you'll be dismissed with scorn
For those who join the faerie race, they must be purely born.
So can you call him evil? this creature of the night?
He only seeks to live his life, and purify his plight.

Bernadette Morris

NIGHT WHISPERS

In the still of the night
many whispers be heard.
Yes the call of the owl
that very wise bird.

Watching there from on high
suddenly swooping down,
On unsuspecting prey
its glory to crown.

Nocturnal creatures stir
from their slumber so deep.
Screeching bats fly around
whilst foxes do creep.

Scavenging in the dark
their orange eyes, so bright.
Badgers too leave their setts
rewards bring delight.

Hedgehogs scurry along
spines ready in defence.
So alert these small chaps
simply no pretence.

Silver moonbeams do shine
tranquillity to share.
How twinkling stars smile
on all life out there.

Margaret Jackson

HIGHLAND NIGHTS

In the Northern Highlands away from the seething crowd,
Night time gathers quickly where rugged peaks stand proud,
As day time melts to darkness far from fear and strife,
Can we compare the solitude to stress of city life.

Towering mountains standing, guarding silent glens,
Haunting, eerie silence, distant brooding bens,
Memories come flooding of mysteries long ago,
Until the morning sun again casts its warming glow.

Sparkling stars are winking, above in cloudless sky,
Darkness hides its secrets, we do not reason why,
City lights seem distant from this serene place,
No footsteps on a pavement, no sound of hurried pace.

The cries of distant wildlife is carried on the breeze,
The soft wind in the darkness whispers in the trees,
Shadows lengthen slowly until daylight comes again,
A curlew sings its plaintive haunting sad refrain.

Around the cottage fire at night chilling tales are told,
Through mists of time and history deeds of old unfold,
In the eerie darkness far from city lights,
Highland folklore wakens in the lonely misty nights.

Alister H Thomson

NIGHT WHISPERS

Dream or reality, a noise awoke me with a start,
my heart leapt a thousand beats
as I lay there, tensed, afraid
to move in case the merest creak
I made should set in motion
a chain of events
over which I had no control.
Looking back in time
I realise now
that on the whole my reaction
was simplistic notion
of self-defence mistaken.
Yet when I awoke to the day
I found a note
slipped just under the door,
and *then* felt shaken . . .
How foolish I felt,
it was but the milkman
leaving my change.

Ann Voaden

FACING FAX

This panic that surrounds me
Has a wholesome, homely feel
Since I've pinched myself hard, twice
To make sure that I'm 'surreal'
Before I wallow in self pity
Pretend I'm Walter Mitty
Call a policeman 'Kitty, Kitty'
Search for seashells in the city . . .

The result has me light headed
Because the horrors that I dreaded
Didn't stop or go away
Once night became another bright new day . . .

Betty Lightfoot

ETERNAL NIGHTS

Journey into tomorrow's dawn
Missing temptation's night,
Purest our human form
Without blackened plight.

Experiences held in darkness
Wear supercilious smiles,
Devil's advocate on your shoulder
Parrot's incessant bark.

Purified lightest shapes,
Cocooned in virgin love,
Shredding vilest capes
Lure symbolic dove.

P Sharp

NIGHT WHISPERS

Now I relax as the sun drifts away,
My mind wakes up as darkness comes to play.
Only for short time as birds begin their call,
Now it is morning, dress and stand tall.
Enjoying the sunshine, with body outstretched
On white sands so wide; the sea will protect.
'But to me night is the best part of the day,
You can wish and dream all your troubles away.'

Janet A Rimmer

THE HAUNTED HOUSE

Determined brave, head held high, I entered no-man's-land.
I turned upon the threshold and shook my dear friend's hand.
'Have no fear for me,' said I 'for I myself have none.
I'll see you in the morning, at the rising of the sun.'

I gazed around the big, old house as dusk began to fall,
At all the creeping shadows rising high upon the wall.
'Poor house,' said I, "'tis such a shame you must live here all alone,
When 'tis only man's irrational fear, that stops you being a *home*.'

To my consternation I heard a man's voice say,
'You're wrong my friend, this is my home, but I welcome you
to stay.'
As the ghost appeared before me, cold fear gripped at my heart,
I bowed, and said, 'I th..th..th..ank you sir, but I really must depart.'

Outside the house, I turned to stare, the sun shone clear and bright,
Did I really see a ghost, or was it just the night?

Penni Nicolson

MOTHER NATURE

Mother Nature brings us many
different things from
cute and cuddly animals
to raging thunderstorms
mists that hover
over moors
desolate and spooky castles and
disruptive avalanches
ready to take lives
Mother Nature
is very unpredictable
and she is there to confuse us
she is kind and gentle one minute
      and
a terrifying devil, next
ready to take you to hell.

J M Stoles

NIGHT INTO DAY

Night reaches out a hand, softly
Covers village, town and country.
Darkness muffles the city streets
And shadows landscape, sky and sea.

An owl stirs, darker wings against dark sky.
Wide-eyed, swoops on its hapless prey.
Bats flutter. The grass sways,
Moved by some creature never seen by day.

Inside tight curtains, people sleep.
Some, with sweet dreams, with wake refreshed tomorrow.
Some toss and turn. Limbs in pain.
Minds still alert; brains analysing sorrow.

But night retires as light takes centre stage.
White clouds dissolve the last stray wisps of grey.
Curtains open, faces peer. Transformation.
Welcome light. Welcome life. Welcome day.

June Ingoldby Holmes

THE TRAIN RAN OVER A HUMAN SLEEPER

A party-goer lay asleep upon a railway line
To slumber off the social fug; well, then the night was fine.
He didn't move a muscle or limb, when a train arrived.
Transport police said they were sure that's why the man survived.

The driver had a feeling he had run somebody down . . .
It had to be a suicide, so he phoned into town -
Then climbed out of the cab, afraid of seeing injuries
Still bleeding. Folk would not take long to think the fault was his!

Police turned up and told the driver to reverse his train
A few yards till they saw the man, who bellowed out in pain.
'You asked for it! You know the railway's not the place to kip
Come to our station, pay at once the fine that's on this slip.'

Gillian C Fisher

My Experience

It was after dark and pouring with rain,
I was walking down a country lane,
A squeal of brakes, a car at my side -
Three young men - I nearly died!

'Want a lift young lady fair?
Oh, I do like your blonde hair!
We can keep you dry - just be calm -
Promise you'll not come to any harm.'

Should I accept or jump the ditch?
I'd always been told 'never to hitch'
I was scared I must admit,
But was tempted too - a little bit!

In ten minutes flat - I was dropped at my door,
I really could not have asked for more.
Three jolly lads, and never a 'hitch'!
I was so glad I'd not jumped the ditch!

Day or night, it is wise to 'beware',
So many dangers lurk everywhere
Just hope that common-sense will prevail,
And you'll still be here, to tell the tale!

Cindy White

THE LAST CHANCE

If the last big bang was coming
and I knew it,
if the hotline rang from God
or the Fates dropped an e-mail
saying 'Twenty-four hours then chop-chop,'
I would seek out the one who needs me,
the one whom the crowds turn away from
because of repellent charmlessness
and honesty.
I would seek that one weeping
on whatever headland,
chained to some lonely rock,
or imprisoned in a tower with dark forests all around.
And if the last big bang was coming
and she knew it,
she would let me coax her out of that trance of grief
with neither my lady-killing ways
nor dazzling good looks,
but with the compassion of those who face the end of things,
with the gentleness and kindness
of an unfavoured mortal.
And when the last big bang came
and we knew it,
we would fly together into God's world
like two small birds
who find shelter in each other
and comfort in an apocalypse.

Colin Mackay

ONE LAST CHANCE

The first siren
The German plane swooping down in daylight in
Camden Town
The landmine back of our house in Medburn Street
The doodle-bugs that suddenly stopped - then
maybe stopped again and came back - *thud*!
Where?
The echo of the bombers, the scare
Waiting for your friends to arrive each morning
after bombings all night
We never had time to think of being in a plight

Imagine all that darkness
And trains full of foot-sloggers with their
rifles today
It certainly was different then
And without Hitler we were so happy

The odd trips in the sunshine in summer
on Sunday or your day in lieu
Happy to have known all of you

Good people - I would like to invite you
No matter how many
You know if you knew me

We at the office were going to meet in
ten years time - but of course, life goes on
I did so miss you
So if 24 hours are all that is left
We should get together
There is so much catching up to do.

Phyllis O'Connell

LIFE WILL FIND A WAY

Of all the things in the world
That I would like to do,
It has to be said that I would
At first have to think it through.
If I discovered that the human race
Had only twenty-four hours to live,
I would think very hard at what
I can take and also what I can give.

There would be lots of things on my mind,
Thinking of all that'll be left behind.

Thinking of the things that I have always wanted
And of all the places I would like to go,
Never going to be able to get those things,
Or of the places I'll never know.
I think that I would sit and ponder
Of what else could have been,
If the world wasn't going to be no longer
And what more we could have seen.

There always has and always will
Be a world of beauty and grace,
There may also be in the future
Some other kind of race.

There is always going to be a future
Even if it is not for us,
There will always be a way to nurture
I know this because:

Meanings have life and life has meaning
And life is meant to be,
So I know there will always be
A place in life for you and me.

Michaela W Garlick

ONE LAST CHANCE

If we should ever get a last chance,
my last 24 hours I would enhance,
sitting in my garden with my cat on my lap,
reflecting on my life and how to face the new 'trap'.
It is too late to buy or to do things . . your life's ambition
soon to be shattered beyond definition!

The fact is, we were never meant to stay on this Earth.
We are only temporary guests, passing through in our search
for purpose, fulfilment and happiness,
as a good citizen, avoiding crime, doing our best!

In my own sweet way,
I am grateful to be here today;
and if that should be my last,
I hope to be able to empty my whisky bottle fast . . .
and drift on.

Annemarie Poole

THE FINAL DAY

What a difference a day makes,
Twenty-four hours till we cease to exist,
No time for regrets,
Just one last chance to make amends,
Take leave of friends.
My scattered brood have all rushed home
For one more get-together,
This is our last, let's make it good,
Yes, one great celebration for what we had.
Life's not been bad - no cause to complain,
There's nothing to gain - pour a libation to the past.

God trusted us with Mother Earth - gave us birth.
We took our fill with little thought of consequence.
Politicians craved more power, enhanced their fame,
Lead us like sheep in their fatal war game
Now all too late, we know the score, there's nothing more.

So raise your glasses to Tony Blair
Likewise his buddy Bill
The Peacemakers, the ones who care
And pound the Earth with bombs and missiles
Killing all at will.
For mankind, no salvation - only nuclear retaliation
Who was right? Who was wrong?
It's too late now to care
We have no hope, there's no last chance
Just silence everywhere.

June Plange

OUR FUTURE

'Tis when there are no longer birds
And silent now the dawning comes,
When no more lions roar the night
And nothing in the moonlight prowls,
No foxes run before the hounds
And nothing rustles underground,
When all the fishes gasp their last
In the poisoned seas.

'Tis then we tell our children
Of the splendid sights we saw
When we were young and curious
And the Earth ran with life,
For they will have the images
That flicker across the screen
Or the sad and lonely animals
That pace the cages of the zoos.

Shall we boast of what we did,
How we made their lives so rich
With gadgets and those extra gifts
Bought with the spoils of progress?
And shall we proudly lecture them
Of what we did for their future,
And what a lovely world we leave
For them to pass to their child?

Richard Reeve

UNCERTAIN PLANET

A poor man can be happy
A rich man maybe sad
A man can make money
But money not the man
A man can know knowledge
But may not know himself
A man can make a life
Or take a life away
'Just add water, stir in life'
A man can show emotion
Or hide it all away
Rain can fall on a summer's day
Sun can shine in winter
A cloud that's lined with silver
A man may grow old
Only to become young again
A man can live a lie
A lie can live a man
Dead leaves will fall in autumn
Springtime, new leaves will grow
Night will follow day
Or day may follow night
Hunger may lead to death
Just like over-eating
Life is about balance
And balance is life
A man may speak in many tongues
But may not know what he is telling
I don't know what I want any more
I no longer know what I hunger for
Such is life on an uncertain planet . . .

Nevin McCloy

LIFE MOVES SO FAST

The more you do, the more you learn
The more varied your life
The more you're able to gain
He makes it so easy for us
Each road laid out like a planned out map.
You can take it slow, or just let go.
But I want to keep up
With this whipped up life.

Like a spinning arrow,
Till it finds the right way to go;
Are my thoughts at the now.
Where I'm heading; I don't yet know.
Like ripples in a river - starting off always so small,
Till you give them chance to grow right out
And from it you soon see results.
Watch it as it circles from just one small stone.
Like arrows, like ripples.
Life moves so fast.

Naomi Elisa Price

THE WANDERING PATH

Seer or prophet the many year
Must know a future near
Whatever our fear or thought
Few escape in the thick net caught
In embraces fateful, tight and sure
That strangle and kill as we struggle more!

'Pon our false world all are agreed
Writ a book for none to read
And few from it freed.
Word 'pon world and horror acumen
A tome to unbalance and not for men.

Anomaly where we seek hope
But only after evil can we grope
And this fair world where once beauty had
It's place by scientific riddle are we waylaid
In cruelties vile and much suffering
In malefic effect seeking praises to sing.

Where visionaries had so long foretold
A light or prophet known of old
Or yet anew can light our path that none knew
And still perhaps followed by the few.
But this is not in numbered victims
Fractured automata of false limbs

Where night is day and nature refracted
Is finally downcast and subtracted
For a planet domiciled in terror
Read in terror to laboratories in error
For such invention can to this empty path lead
Where all is possible and none to real life or hope can concede.

John Amsden

Realism

Go for organic gardening!
Create a compost heap -
But be aware, slugs will live there,
And breed while you're asleep.

Please recycle everything!
The tip is no solution -
But mind that the recycling
Might mean much more pollution.

Eat less fat! Take exercise!
Your willpower should be stronger -
But when you live on lettuces
You don't want to live longer.

Enough advice! To hell with it!
Let's go for hedonism -
And when life's paltry pleasures pall
We'll practice pessimism.

Barbara Beaumont

THE PIRATE OF THE HOLY GRAIL

To the theatre - the theatre - say I?
The theatre of the mind?
A new frontier?
I had been there before
But only fragments of memory remained.
Now, I was aware of The Pirate
That rocked and steadied on its glide
To ride through space and time
Beyond the climes of the world
I had left behind
To the souls that lived
In a new world's atmosphere.
I held on for dear life.
I would see my Father, others -
Magdalene and Christ, who had died
In the agony of the world governments' style
That categorised and defined the mind
To provide
An attitude of abstract, dual-thinking
In a tyranny of government 'ideals'
That bore no relation
To Einstein's Theory of Relativity
Or the force of The Pirate
That embodied reality
That was supersonic.
A New Order had been introduced
And it knew no life - death counterpoint
As a conceptual device.
The force was recognised as the Holy Grail of Life
When I travelled The Pirate in 2099.

David de Pinna

DOMINO EFFECT

The world's weather has started to change,
With results, both diverse and strange,
Years of drought, now lots of rain,
Clogging mud and washed away grain.

Africa, India, Australia and the USA,
Have been almost scorched away,
Rising oceans, causing much disaster,
Land masses, disappearing faster.

Icecaps melting, water cooling fast,
Which, in turn, causes snow and icy blast,
Countries which have never known cold,
Are seeing snow, with blizzards unfold.

More volcanoes are active, at this time,
Belching ash and lava, and hot slime,
Poison gases, darkening skies to grey,
And global warming, is here to stay.

Earthquakes follow, bringing fear and dread,
Which changes the course of a river bed,
Brush fires, causing so much smoke,
Causing towns and cities to choke.

Sun spots, bringing very high gales,
Much flooding this entails,
Computers have been known to flop,
Confidence, in these will stop.

Robert Thompson

IS THE WORLD GOING TO COME TO A STANDSTILL?

I wonder what's going to happen in the year 2000.
Are we not going to make a cup of tea,
Or ever switch the TV on.
Is the world going to come to a standstill?

Babies being born, hospital full.
Shops have to close, while people have fun.
There'll be street parties,
Fireworks, people getting drunk.

Then when all the fun is over and reality sets in
Is it going to make a better world,
Or is it going to flop?
Are *all* the people going to be kinder
To each other?
Are there still going to be wars?
Are we going to be worse off
Or is money going to flow?

Are all the computers going to crash down?
Is day going to be night, or night going to be day?
Are all the seasons going to alter?
Is the ozone going to change.

This we will have to see.
Are all the birds and animals going to get confused?
I feel I'm very pessimistic,
My thoughts are all mixed up.
I'll leave it to the Lord above,
For He will sort it out.

Jean Rickwood

NIGHT WHISPERS

It is quiet, everything is still
The dark, black velvet of night is all around
The house creaks, is someone there?
Maybe it's spirits come to visit.
My imagination is running riot
Am I dreaming or awake?
The solitude of the slumbering world
penetrates my mind, refusing my right to sleep.
I hear it again that noise.
Why does the house creak at night,
never in the daylight hours?
How come the darkness makes familiar places
seem so strange and brooding, like a different
world to one of light?
In the deep of night
I feel no fear as I lay alone.
The darkness wraps around my being
like a soft blanket.
My eyelids close, peaceful sleep
is seconds away.
Tomorrow there will be light.

B Bowles

My Last Night

My last night - my last night
I'll love with all my heart
I'll love and love; my love and I
We'll love into the night.

I'll lay me down on my own bed
I'll think of all gone by
I'll think of all my loved ones - gone
And hope to meet them when I die.

My love and I, we'll cuddle up
What else is there to do?
No need to cook or clean the fridge
All this a waste of time.

I'll lay me down and slumber on
To wake up in a better land
My love and I together - our loved
Ones so to meet.

The sounds in the street mean not a jot
I feel a flutter in my heart
My love and I, how deep we loved
As we prepare to go.

Yet in the morn - if all this was a dream
I might wake up - still in this world
My baby by my side.

Janet Cavill

24 Hours

24 hours,
How long a last day?
Time only for the words
That we hesitate to say.
Hope - for a phone line
To those distanced - forever,
Hope for warm arms . . .
That for brief hours we'll treasure.
Hope for your loved ones . . .
For mankind's survival,
Hope against hope
For our world's revival.
Hope for acceptance . . .
As endless night nears
Hope for forgiveness and
Release from our fears.
Hope - optimistic . . .
As the minutes tick by . . .
Prayers for each other . . .
Lest a last breath we sigh.

Gail Walker

A Ticket To Mars

Twenty-four hours left for the human race!
That should wipe the smile off its fatuous face.
As for me, I am heading away into space;
Yes, I've got a ticket to Mars.

The spaceship blasts off just before it gets light;
Mankind has no future, but mine's looking bright.
What I'm getting at, Jack, is that I am all right,
'Cos I've got a ticket to Mars.

And when I get near to the end of the mission,
Just where I should land is the hardest decision;
The spaceship must touch down with greatest precision,
Or I've wasted my ticket to Mars.

I wonder if Martian food includes roast beef . . .
Oi, mate; tell me quickly: did you see the thief?
I haven't much time, so make your answer brief -
What swine stole my ticket to Mars?

Roger Williams

DARKNESS OF NIGHT

May the darkness of night
Soon fade away
And darkness change
Into a glorious day.

A day so full of love
And sunshine so bright,
It chases away
All fears of the night.

May the angels of God,
Guard us through the night
To keep us safe from harm
Till dawn's early light.

Doreen A Swann

WHEN I WAS YOUNG

My Canadian stepfather
Used to sit me on his knee,
And sing a French-Canadian song
Especially for me.
That old tune was 'Alouette',
And whenever I hear it sung,
I think of that man with a heart of gold,
Who sang it when I was young.

Ivy Neville

AFTERNOON TEA

We all look forward
To Thursday tea
With Phyllis and May
Who make anyone's day
There's Janet, Pat and Jackie,
Sheila and Rosemary,
Just to name a few.
All giving time voluntarily
Oh! And Jill with her marmalade too.
They bake us cakes
Cheese scones and tarts
And sometimes show us photographs
There's always someone
With a story to tell
And sometimes Happy Birthday as well.
We have a chat
About this and that
And sometimes get a doggy bag
There's an added bonus
When Vicar joins us
But all too soon the clock strikes four
And home we have to go once more
But we all look forward with glee
To the next Thursday afternoon tea.

Rosalie Wells

TO A LONG-LOST FRIEND

When life has long forgotten me,
And my ramblings at last have ceased,
Think only this of me, my friend,
When all my innermost thoughts released,
That I had found a true serenity,
Of the deepest calibre ever found,
And drank in life's sweetest moments,
Long before you, or I, might be renowned.

And when you pause to recall my name,
Will puzzlement fill your brow?
For *you* never knew how much I cared,
How could you know my earnest vow,
To find you and hold your hand
Just once more,
As we did when our hearts beat as one?
So remember me,
For my gloriously happy days,
Knowing I'll meet you again,
When, at last, our lives are done.

Julia Eva Yeardye

THE WAY OF LIFE

Is this happiness when you wake with fear each day?
Conquer it how you may.
When children are born whose loyalties are torn
Try to strive for perfection.
The day of conception
Other people's troubles you share
As true friends are rare.
Trouble and strife through rugged pathways of life.
Murder, rape, greed and envy
What caused this hate?
Families to you relate.
When loved ones deteriorate before your eyes
One gets on with life and sighs.
Could it be man's self-destruction?
Drugs, greed and corruption.
Poverty, homelessness and despair.
Is a free meal degrading?
In fine frocks parading.
Do they turn the other way
Hoping the problem will go away?
We are all guilty of this.
Our thoughts do we dismiss?
To feel the state of the world today
Come survive what may
Is life just a rose on a thorn?
Our making a decision like a pawn.

Ann Dutschak

PASSING OF A FRIEND

Silently in church we wait
To pay our last respects
Our friend who battled valiantly,
In life - had no regrets.
The great door slowly opened,
With the organist on cue
All bearers dark and sombre,
As we rose up from the pew.
Their vicar leads the mourners,
His voice rings loud and clear
'I am the Resurrection' -
- So death will hold no fear.
The hymns that have been chosen
Well-known to us you see,
First to the tune of 'Crimmond',
Close with 'Abide With Me'.
We knelt and prayed together
Some 'old', some 'very young'
Tears for our friend were evident
His last journey had begun!
So onward to interment
At the grave we say 'Farewell,'
Surely we shall meet again
In the House of the Lord, will dwell!

T G Bloodworth

HE LOVES ME REALLY

She's here again, that woman of mine,
Doesn't speak, she hasn't the time.
She's busy dragging the hoover out,
'Plug it in pet,' I hear her shout.
There's washing strewn all over the floor,
I'd give her a lift, but my back's still sore.
She's upstairs now changing the bed,
I wish she'd stop, she's doing my head.
She's in and out like a deranged bat,
There's one thing for sure, she'll never be fat.
The ironing all neatly folded in a pile,
That's that done! She says with a smile.
Off to school to pick up our son,
Ah! A woman's work is never done.
I think I'll go and peel her some spuds,
On second thoughts, I'll shower and change my duds.
Tea's ready! It's on the table,
Get out the knives and forks if you're able.
Oh! She's stopped now rushing around,
Emmerdale on so don't make a sound.
It's nine o'clock, time for a brew,
You make it love, while I go to the loo.
Go to bed dear, I won't be a minute,
It'll just be warm by the time I get in it.
I climb into bed she's asleep already,
I love her really 'cause she's better than me teddy.

Linda Woodhouse

TOTIES TWO YEARS ON

The Toties have been in power for two years now
And they dominate the Scots Parliament and Welsh Assembly too
The Toties haven't a true majority in Scotland or Wales
But they seem to act as though they do.

The Toties and the Lib Dems or Todies
Are trying to join forces in the new Parliaments
The Toties and Todies running Scotland and Wales
With the Nationalists into Opposition sent.

Soon there will be calls for an English Parliament
But the Toties don't want to know
Perhaps based in Birmingham or Manchester
Will the Toties be made to create one so?

Or there be Assemblies
In different English regions and areas
In Bristol, Leeds, Nottingham, etc
The break-up of England soon, one fears.

A disunited Queendom
United under the Toties
Starting with the Third Millennium
In partnership with the Todies.

H G Griffiths

THE WASHING CYCLE

I'm in the womb floating slowly round,
Turning amongst the gentle sounds.
Next I'm lowered in tender arms,
Washed and bathed a soothing calm
A little older and splashing all,
I squeal with delight, I'm two foot tall.
As my mind and body starts to grow,
There's monsters deep and sharks below.
Then comes the time, to put toys away,
To do other things than sit and play.
I clean and scrub, I'm at that age,
There's a need to smell nice, it's just a phase.
As life goes on and with candles glowing,
The hot steam rising, the water flowing,
I lie relaxed in my mountain of bubbles
And ease away life's little troubles.
Now I'm old and creak with pain.
I reflect back, upon all life's gains.
I think about my chosen path,
While I drift away in my hot bath!

Karen Hollinghurst

HE'S WON THE CUP!

The golf was going smoothly - now at the final hole,
Amateur golfer playing fairly - but loose came his shoe sole,
Others doing better - but he'd enjoyed the fun,
Had had an average round - out there in the sun,
A bit behind on scoring - professional the others were,
Young lad chose a driver - as that he did prefer,
Prepared himself for tee shot - with serious intent,
Hoped with trusty driver 'twould fall near refreshment tent,
That was near that last hole - where play would finish up,
Played a perfect tee shot - landed plop in a teacup!

John L Wright & 'Jackdaw'

A STRANGER WITHIN

You gave up your life to care for me,
I sense your sadness every day,
I see the hope fade in your eyes,
That things won't always be this way.

I watch you with all the love,
That I had the day we met,
My love for you grows stronger,
And with each day stronger yet.

I feel the love you have for me,
With each tender word you say,
To have you spend your time with me,
Makes life worth another day.

I know you'd love to enjoy life,
To feel young and once more free,
You never blame anyone for your life,
The life you gave to me.

I'd never blame you if you left,
I know you find it hard to cope,
I see in your eyes your sadness,
Though you say you live in hope.

Hope is something I have lost,
My body is a stranger to me,
I no longer see the person I was,
But your love sets me free.

Siobhan Cleary

ANOTHER WEEK

Here we go again into another week,
Wondering what's going to happen,
Will it be sad or happy?
Life's full of surprise and worry,
So take your time and do not hurry.

Enjoy every moment either good or bad,
You were made to get involved,
And at the end of the week,
You'll say, 'It wasn't too bad after all,
And I've learnt quite a lot,'
So, next week, try and be more bold and confident.

Kenneth Mood

TIME

'Where did the morning go?'
I often hear you say.
'What happened to Winter?'
As Spring is on the way.

Sometimes a minute lasts
Forever more it seems.
Does time go the same speed
At night-time during dreams?

Often folk will ring you,
'When are you coming down?'
It seems like yesterday,
You lunched with them in town.

You meet friends from the past,
The years have soon rolled by.
It's twenty years or more,
They do say time can fly.

Each second of each day,
Deserves a lot of thought,
So spend your time wisely,
For time cannot be bought.

Angela Pritchard

MY CAB DRIVER

He turned the music up for me, life boring.
'These are still the good times.'
She is saying goodbye to her successful son.
I'm a survivor, I'm hungry.

Life wants to clear you,
I got arrested by a man and woman cop.
'He can't help it.'
I've chosen to live.
It's strange how we follow our psychological patterns.

Alan Cornelius

BACK TO SCHOOL

I went back to school
everything had changed,
Lucy had a new pencil case
my class, was on their
twelve times table
everything had changed.
The school had a new
guinea pig,
there was a new kid
in my class
my teacher had had a baby!
Everything had changed.
My mates all had new uniforms,
the school dinners
weren't as good
assembly was still
as boring,
Well!
Not everything had changed.

Tanya McCollum

EACH CHIEFLY

The drone,
Of a plane.
The scream,
Of a child.
The soft touch,
Of a song.

A moment,
And strands;
Each,
Chiefly,
In its lessons.

Distance,
So flung;
Tamed only,
By boldness.

Need,
Too acute,
For neglect.

Persuasions,
So ripe;
Succumb,
Noble.

Each,
Chiefly,
In its lessons.

Rio

THE GARDEN OF ECHOES

Quietly I opened the old iron gate,
Its rusty hinges grind and grate.
Latch in my hand I pause in my tracks,
Shall I go in or shall I turn back?
For here is a garden, its beauty still shows
That someone had cared and loved long ago.
Down a leafy-strewn path I carried on,
To find myself near a garden pond.
Once it had rippled, peaceful, serene.
Now it was filled with dead fallen leaves.
An angel face cherub has caught my eye
Peeping through the prickly briar.
Did I imagine I heard a deep sigh
That came as a murmur on a breeze passing by?
Or was it an echo of a lover's goodbye
As they whispered their love would never die?
With one last look I turn to go
And leave behind my gardens of echoes.

E F Parker

THE DALES

I love to walk among the Dales,
Of England's prettiest shire,
And step out in the wind and gales -
Harsh winter in full ire!
For I have made this land my own,
Her every beaten path,
Leaping every stepping stone,
Every river's birth;
And I have sat within her shades,
In paradise for free,
Where waters glide within her glades,
Close by each willow tree;
And I have sought more hidden ways,
Where seldom men have gone,
And stood on hills that I might gaze,
As the evening sun goes down.

What is it about the Dales . . .
So unique in their own way?
Is it greater beauty that prevails . . .
Than the Yukon or Yosimite?
The adornment of the Pyrenees. . .
The Dolomites by chance!
The turquoise colour of Eilat . . .
The warmth of southern France?
The rolling hills of Tuscany . . .
The windswept coast of Maine!
The autumn gold of Loch Katrine . . .
The aridness of Spain?
You can show me all of a thousand sights . . .
And argue all you can!
But this little piece of England's delights . . .
Just draws me back again.

Tom Ritchie

SHEPHERD'S DELIGHT

Along leafy lanes of Summer
With my sweetheart I did go,
Hand-in-hand we strolled together
With lazy steps and slow.

Mid-winter when we last met,
The months slipped slowly by,
I am virtuous and chaste now,
Explaining with a sigh.

We watched the fiery sunset,
And kissed like lovers do,
My cool response subdued him,
As from me he withdrew.

He took me in his arms again,
His words were warm and tender,
As sun was sinking westward
No sky could match his ardour.

Gazing long upon his sad face,
His blue eyes shone with candour,
A lump now came into my throat,
He had pierced through my languor.

So suddenly my heart gave way
In the dusky evening light,
Love broke through my shy reserve,
I belonged to him that night.

Betty Mealand

I'll Still Love You

I'll be here she'd often say
Until time takes our love away.
Now in each other's lives we play our part
I live in your life while you're here in my heart.
There are those amongst us who say
Live your life for each passing day.
Just enjoy your time together
As if it was your last.
Life's full of changing seasons
They all go by so fast.
She'd often say come tomorrow
I may have to go but I will be
Richer for having loved you
More than you will ever know.
A little love goes a long way
And I will still remember you
When I'm far away
I'll still be in your memories
You will still be in mine.
I'll be in those night-time stars
Following you wherever you go.
You will be the love I left behind.
But I'll still love you more than
               you will ever know.

K Lake

CLOCKING OUT

The message that my brain received
Was stop those legs from running
For the heart is beating fast
And the lungs are very cunning.
Don't eat so much my stomach cried
Fat foods are not digestive.
You read too many romance books
Put down, your eyes need resting.
Switch off that noise my eardrums roared
I've stood enough, the limit.
And from the skin and angry pores
Turn down the fire this minute.
I've had enough my forehead said
For goodness' sake get off to bed.
So all of us can sleep and rest
To face tomorrow's endurance test.

J Wren

WHAT WAS THAT DREAM?

In the wee small hours I had this dream
Was it all that it did seem?
I was walking in some open space
With a man whom I did not know his face.
As through that large garden we both did walk
To flocks of birds the man did talk.
In body safe tucked up in my bed
Yet in dreams, seagulls above my head.
Then something I did not understand
On a fence a small angel did land
With snow-white wings, off it took
And landed at the man's foot and started to look.
For I felt such a fool
As it was my name it did then call
What has made it speak to me
And how could this thing possibly be?
Could this dream have been so true
And that angel me he knew?
As spirit friends to my heart I will take
That strange dream ended when I did awake.

Colin Allsop

WITHOUT YOU

How do you feel
In different situations?
Maybe you love me
In different imitations.
It's love you say,
He's earned his pay
As for me, I stand alone.

P Allen

WE DECIDE

Is life a dream?
A dream we do not appreciate?
Is it a test for our capabilities?
What if it is?
What if we *are* judged
So when we wake up we'll be in heaven,
Or hell.
We were all born to the test,
But to prove ourselves we must
                help our environment,
Our world,
Not destroy it,
We are destroying it,
Destroy is a strong word,
And yet it does not describe what we have and *are*
doing,
Murder is another word.
We are all capable of passing the test,
But do we want to use our capabilities?
We are becoming too idle
To even understand our faults,
So do we murder or help,
Heaven or Hell?

We decide the future of our planet,
The future *is* in your hands,
What do you decide?

      Heaven or Hell?

Alice Michell (12)

A World For The Future

In the future,
In the future,
What will our world be like?
No trees or bees,
And no spring breeze,
No plants or animal life.

In the future,
In the future,
Will we still be here?
Will we still be on this planet,
It's death that we now fear.

In the future,
In the future,
Will everything grow back?
We've cut down all the trees and plants,
We've even stamped on ants!

In the future,
In the future,
What will we see?
Just another barren planet
No life, no nothing,
Not even the sea.

In the future,
In the future,
How can we change our planet's future?
Put back all the plants and trees,
And try to stop global warming . . .
                                    please!

Georgina Forrest (12)

ENVIRONMENT

Beautiful flowers, plants and trees,
Flying flies and buzzing bees.
Bees make honey, wasps may sting,
With the birds as they may sing.

Squirrels scuttling across the ground,
Crafty foxes cannot be found.
Mice are running, spiders are crawling,
Cats and dogs may be calling.

But this fine world is being destroyed,
By bulldozers making noise.
Ruining fields chopping down trees,
Nowhere to live for the birds and bees.

This fine world that we live in,
Some people want to throw in the bin.
Building shops, destroying homes,
Treating animals like garden gnomes.

This is what it's like in our world,
I'd think you'd agree it is *absurd!*

Jonathon Simons (11)

A World For The Future?

Day after day,
Tree after tree,
Home after home,
Man destroys what we see.

Hunt after hunt,
Shot after shot,
Death after death,
Wildlife left to rot.

Police after police,
Crime after crime,
Jail after jail,
Not so clever this time.

Filth after filth,
Dirt after dirt,
Pain after pain,
I think God is hurt!

Tambi Maple

THE FUTURE?

Synthetic, cosmetic,
Rubber trees, man-made breeze,
This is what the future sees.

Implants, transplants,
Computer brains take the reins,
Spaceships will replace the planes.

Giant screens, laser beams,
Yellow skies, wildlife dies.
Government lies, while the planet cries.

Is this to be the future?
Advanced yet in distress,
Some people can't care less
So let's withstand the test
Let's not pollute the world.

Simon Barlow

AFTER THE STORM

Rain dripping, beating the concrete floor,
Making small oceans on the ground,
Drumming, softly then loudly,
On the window frame, making a horrible
Slapping sound.

Darkened grey clouds, looking down,
If touched would release water, the size
of an ocean.
Flooding everything in its path,
In one terrible motion.

The sun has returned, after months of showers,
Such a heartening sight,
Golden rays engulf the place,
Seeping through the window,
Filling everything around with a
feeling of grace.

Kimberly Harries

Philosophy

If you wonder what made you the way you are;
The person of today.
Fatalistic. Realistic. Hound to culture's way.
Then you'll create a something new,
And maybe, yet, another you.
But all this mental, thoughtful change
Will not itself expand your range.
Will adding to a purer sorrow,
Make a different self tomorrow?

Martin Buckley

IF I WON THE LOTTERY

To have the very best of everything,
new clothes, house and car,
holidays in abundance, shopping
trips near and far. Oh what fun
could be had, it couldn't be as bad
as some folk seem to think, to be
forever 'in the pink'.

To go tell the boss, 'I don't give a toss!'
Buy designer gear, never having to fear
any bills that may come my way, now I
can pay.

To treat one's fellows with things of good
cheer, good food, wine and beer.
Holidays abroad for good friends of mine
that stayed by me all the time.

It would be like Christmas every day,
fair-weather friends can stay away.
I know whom to trust, no words of
gloom can ever spoil my pleasure with
their prophesies of doom.

Never to work from 9 to 5, nor toil
after hours like a bee in a hive.
To be free to enjoy the simple things
in life, a free spirit travelling
along life's way, cushioned from the worries
that used to spoil my day. There would never
be any monotony, not if I won the Lottery!

Jill Johnson

POEM ABOUT MAUREEN

My friend Maureen, a great friend to me
always walks so close to God
she always feels him near
no matter what's she's trusted him
through the years
and see you through he surely does
each second, each minute, each year, he's close to you Maureen
because you're like a peaceful dove
on a mission of happiness
and spreading your love to people in need and for those you love
spreading love and happiness, always doing good deeds
in memory of your beloved daughter, you give so much in life
a flower in a world where
there's too much hate and greed
Maureen is an inspiration to us all indeed
you are a loyal friend to me.

D McDonald

THE JUICE OF NATURE!

He sticks in my mind
Like a sucked sticky sweet,
He reminds me of a hot sunny season,
When the birds go tweet!

His motions are swift,
Like a smooth-flying bird,
He makes an impact on my life,
Like a trampling herd!

The flowers grow,
But never die,
Like the love
I have for him and I!

Fresh fruit reminds me
Of our love,
The juices of nature,
They were sent from above!

Our love won't end,
That's what I pray,
But will we come apart?
Maybe, some day!

Natalie Iley

THE ROSE

When I look in the mirror,
What do I see?
Pain and anger
Of what once was a rosebud,
But then a weed grew up from the soil,
At first sight it seemed to be unhurtful,
Then it was watered.
It grew to the heart of the rose,
And strangled the roots of a strong friendship,
Then the death of the roots reached the heart,
The love and care that we once gave to each other.
All that is left of the rose,
Is a fossil,
Buried deep in the ground,
The fossil of a friendship,
That will never be seen again.

Heather Rowley (12)

BABY BLUES

I smile with relief at Baby's cry
Precious - precious breath of life
A bond never to be torn
Such innocence in my first-born - my first-born . . .

Then my eyes open and I shut them tight
Trying to keep my dream alive
I'm so exhausted from the heartache and pain
For the little kicks I'll always crave
It stays with me day and night
No one knows the river I cry
For every woman the whole world through
Who has to bear - the baby blues!

I pound my fist in the earth
In frustration and despair
For those who can and those who can't
The divide is deep and it's too far
But I pray to walk in their shoes
To find a cure for these baby blues.
These Baby Blues!

Frank Howarth-Hynes

GOODBYE

I love it when you laugh,
I love it when you smile,
That's what makes my time
With you so worthwhile.

I hate it when you're upset,
I hate it when you start to regret,
That's because I hate seeing
you unhappy.

I love it when you tell stories,
I love it when you tell me jokes,
That's because I love you the most.

I hate it when you start to cry,
I hate it when you give up and don't try,
But most of all, I hate saying 'Goodbye.'

Sahdia-Sarah Suraiyya (13)

MUSIC IS IN THE AIR

Oh! There are worthier themes for poet's pen
In this great hour secret feels the shame
When music sounds, gone is the Earth I know
Messages come from the mystic sphere.

Is it the harp that fairy fingers
Sweep to charm us with its tone
It is the happy hour of pleasant echo
The voices of their household band.

The heathery heights in vision rise
Though I toil through the day for precarious food
With my body worn down and my spirit subdued
We often destroy the present joy for future hope.

Sadly sweet in day's decline
To mark the waning sun
And make all beauteous things and golden hour
But words are found with melody tunes.

Heather Aspinall

PASSING TIME

Time itself can play many parts - time to think and work it out - time to enjoy days of life - other times to ponder on failed events - a time to laugh - a time to fill our eyes with tears - how true the reasoning - we who are living on this earth are all ruled by the passing of time itself - a time of birth - a time of life until we reach the time of death - that can be likened to an early morning mist - it appears then disappears from view - with thoughts like this in mind we should hold high the value, the passing hours of each passing day - use our gift of sight to see the beauty on this globe - and find time to try to understand what this life is really all about - find time to believe there is a God above - believe - that He has allowed your life from your day of birth - understand that you are a wonder that was never here before - time has many ways - a time to gain - a time to lose - time to reflect on passing events - whilst time itself moves forward - time itself will not go back again - with thoughts like this in mind - I am well aware that life itself is a gift made up of time - and time itself one day will pass me by.

R P Scannell

MY THOUGHTS OF BOYS

There are two boys I know called,
Russell and Luke, they're nice and generous,
They are also really good
                    but...
I've got three brothers
One, very very kind,
Another, he is quite nice,
The youngest, he's a pain
He gets me in trouble but I suppose he's OK . . .

I would not be here if it weren't for my dad
'Cause he was once a boy.

Also Russell and Luke live near me
And go to my school,
I'm in Year 7 and they're in Year 8.
So, overall boys are great, they're
                    ten out of ten, AOK!

Kayleigh Rosewarne (11)

BOYS

Boys, they're so dumb!
They play football and say
They know everything
About it, but when you ask
Them a question,
They get it wrong!

In class when the teacher
Asks them an *easy* question,
They go and get it wrong.

At lunch, when you're eating
They start talking about
Something that is totally
Gross and make you feel
Sick!

Boys! They're so disgusting!

Nicola Strapp-Freeman (10)

BOYS

I like my daddy.
I don't like boys because
boys hurt me.
I love my dad because
he buys me stuff.
Boys are silly
Boys are silly-billy boys
They play silly football
Boys have different haircuts
Boys talk different
Boys are different in every way.

Emma Rigden (10)

TAKE BOYS

Take boys,
My brother for example,
Annoying, tedious,
And a very big handful.

Take men,
My father for example,
Tall, funny,
And very, very handsome.

Take blokes,
My friend for example,
Tall, skinny,
And very, very thankful.

I think that boys are a mix,
That's why girls find it so hard
To pick!

Felicity Anne Carter

THE BOY

Who's annoying,
Argues with you
And always thinks they're right?

Who's always in the bathroom before school,
Makes you late
And stinks the bathroom out with their cheap aftershave?

Whose bedroom is always in a tip
And socks smell like rotten eggs being left in the sun for a year?

Who's handsome,
Caring,
Kind and considerate?
They're always there when you need them.

Who thinks they're hard,
Spits,
And walks with their mutinated gang?

Who's the one you love
And the one you love to hate?

It's that creature called a . . . Boy!

Natasha Clarke

GIRLS ON BOYS

Boys like football,
Boys like football,
Boys are sometimes good,
And sometimes naughty.

On the way home the boys run out of the bus,
Out of the bus!
Out of the bus!
Out of the bus!

Catherine Manderson (7)

GIRLS ON BOYS

They sit there flicking all day,
'You stupid boys' the teacher says!
The teacher says 'Go to the headmaster!'
'Oh! Oh!' says one of the boys, 'This is a disaster!'
The headteacher says 'You're such a danger to all the class,
Oh and about your exams, you will never pass!
It is possible that I will cut your head off,
Or on the other hand, I might chain you up in my dark loft!'
I've lost my patience with you boys,
I will tell your mothers not to get you any toys.
Now go back to class, be nice to the teacher,
I don't want to hear that you have to come to me,
The headteacher!'

Mary Poynter (8)

UNTITLED

I often think of lands so fair,
Green trees and skies of blue.
But I know I'll never get there,
This I know is true.
I'm stuck here, trapped within these walls,
Of brick and stone and sand.
Never to escape from here,
Built by a human hand.
Green trees are mine, but in my dreams,
Is where the seeds do grow.
Blue skies I see from far away,
On the wrong side of my window.
A prisoner here, in this blackened land,
Of pollution, smoke and chains,
That bound my wrists and ankles tight
To the earth and all its pain.
We kill our trees and burn our fields,
Our oceans are unclean.
And over this the buildings lay,
Black, heartless and mean.
To our poor land this torture comes,
This pollution comes and stands,
So no longer can we sing about
England's pleasant lands.

Anne-Marie Toth (14)

A WORLD FOR THE FUTURE
GOOD/BAD

Good.

A world for the future
Is where animals roam free,
And birds can sing from every tree.

A world for the future
Is where forests grow tall,
And stand where they will never fall.

A world for the future
Is where people are kind,
And peace is the only thing on their mind.

Bad.

A world for the future
Is where seas are black,
And fish die of clean water lack.

A world for the future
Is where pollution kills all,
And builds up a great big litter wall.

A world for the future
Is where war rules us all,
And people fight till they fall.

Amy Frances White

PIG RABBIT EAR

The Pig Rabbit Ear was a southerner
On the pier.
Soon he will die with the spy.
Do you know . . . I love him so!
And he lived in Africa
With his wife. In Africa?

Sally McLardy (10)

Consumatum Est

I have no need of friendship
Nor confident to trust with my heart,
Or pal to cause laughter, at audible quips
Of mankind's unsavoury practices - I wish no part.
Happiness is a game of chance.

I have prayed fervently for release,
But to no avail. I guess there must be a valid reason.
Lord I would be indebted to know why I am not at peace.
Give me an explanation why I shouldn't escape this prison.
Happiness is a game of chance.

It is not the length of life that's important, but the quality
That is paramount to sustain an even balance.
I ache for my life to be over. It's my only priority,
For illness has stolen away my quality of life.
Happiness is a game of chance.

J Baker

THE JOURNEY

'It saves energy,' said simple young Hugh
'To walk slowly or take the bus Miss Blue
I'm clever you see
I save both ways,' said he
'I walk slowly up and down the journey through!'

Joan Wylde

NIGHT WIND

The wind sighs so heavy
In the darkness of the night,
What does it say to you - and to me?
Does it rock you to sleep?
Or as the wind groans do you weep?

The wind so angry but oh so sad,
Tearing at the house and my heart,
A sound of wild loneliness, strangely mad,
What does the wind say? Why does it start
All those strange thoughts in my head?

The night encircles me, a night so deep,
The storm and darkness bring sorrow
And that strange unknown fear,
I search for answers,
But am only denied the comfort of sleep.

Now is the time for loving arms to hold me,
A voice to whisper I am dear,
But there is no voice, only darkness,
The sighing sad wind
And that old familiar unknown fear.

Florence Andrews

170-ODD CANDLES ON THE CAKE?

Why do you think we'll be different
a hundred years from now?
I really doubt it very much,
we'll just be the same, somehow.

Women will still produce babies,
(who'd want a Dolly-like clone?)
and we'll still eat our meat and veggies,
and, by that time, beef on the bone!

We'll still be living in houses,
not holes in the ground, I'm sure.
The rich will be even richer,
and the poor will still be poor.

The scraps will go on around the world,
because man will *never* learn!
And we'll still go out in the sunshine
and regret it when we start to burn!

Our skirts will go higher (or lower)
as we follow some future Dior,
and we'll still grumble the same old grumbles,
and demand for our lot more and more.

We *may* have a few new refinements
like a robot to help 'bout the house,
and instant and *speedy* replacements
should we have as much as a grouse.

But whether I'm right, or whether I'm wrong,
it just will not affect me -
I *doubt* that I'll live as long as that,
so - I won't be here to see!

Joyce Hockley

THE BURGLAR

I woke with a start, kept quiet as a mouse
As someone outside broke into my house.
I'd fallen asleep while watching TV
And now I was trapped unable to breathe.
The thief was next door, he'd broken a pane.
I tried to get up but struggled in vain
My muscles had locked, set rigid in fright.
What a 'to do' if he turned on the light!
Then came a surprise, the thief lost his head.
He let out a sneeze to waken the dead.
Now *he* became scared, his thieving discovered.
He fled. I sat up, composure recovered.
I thought for a bit on what had occurred.
Then smiled to myself, curled up and just purred!

Andrew Mackie

WANTON LOVE

He rose from my warm bed, this lad,
just as dawn broke, sweet birdsong starting.
Broad shouldered, strong, lithe, still unclad,
my memory of the time before his parting.

I never knew from where he came,
just that we had some empathy,
some kindred spirit set aflame,
a gentle time, not needing constancy.

My urge to meet again came with the spring,
I waited through long hours of aching time,
then just as all sweet thoughts of him grew dim
he came, this carefree youth, with love sublime.

Pam Gibbons

BEING DISABLED

I've been disabled now
For many years
It brings many tears and fears
A mobility car, they allowed me
It's so good to get out
Not stuck in on a lovely day
It's so good to get about.

Orange badges I have them,
But they don't do me much 'good'
When I got the 'badges'
I always thought they 'would'
Double yellow lines, I can park on
But I have to get out the car.
It doesn't matter to traffic wardens
With bad legs. I can't walk far.

A carer I have one
Who can stop in the car
But I can't so the traffic warden says
Even on really bad days.

Soaking wet and windswept
Is how I've sometimes been
I wish people, who make these laws
Can understand how silly they seem.

Trisha Moreton

LIFE'S MISFORTUNE

Describe to me a wounded soul
let all who taunt be wary.
Truths laid down to heal the fall
cruel pains are all so many.

Burdened by a righteous thirst
envy hath no natural predator
writer of the soul's bare verse
this blight of man to malice his better.

Enjoy the dancing of the sun
when gloomy days hang heavy
as boisterous streams deceive their run
mine own heart craves for me.

I do recall golden moons that taunt with evening song
and in their play feigning for youth my valour.
Poor soul dreams all undone
come death true heart do favour.

It is now that fashions happiness
glory be shed life's misleading
heed nature's call from heaven blessed
true as now, pain's not this relieving.

'Tis me, yes me, devoid of bliss
is this all done for mortal man
who challenges death's unknown abyss
Embracing the ultimate strength
this humble soul can.

Mansel

A True Friendship

I was referred to a Nottingham hospital
Where to my horror! Breast cancer was diagnosed,
But thanks to the wonderful doctors and nurses
The book of my life wasn't closed.

This is the time when I met Margaret
(Who was to become my very dear friend),
We were to share a room in hospital
For six weeks, which slowly did wend.

I was feeling very ill, and scared at the time,
But Margaret soon put a stop to that,
Remarking, just how lucky we were
Being able, even to just sit and chat.

She often used to say to me,
'It's no use thinking, why me?
There are many patients who are very much worse'
Of course she was right, I did agree.

After that, I didn't feel so full of self pity
And adjusted a little easier at last,
Thankful that I was in such a caring place,
I thought of the future, instead of the past.

Margaret really boosted my ego,
No feeling sad while she was around,
Always caring, and a smile for all,
And yes! Our friendship today is still sound.

Joan A Anscombe

BOYS (FROM A GIRL'S POINT OF VIEW)

Boys are hard to figure out,
As all they do is scream and shout
Stupid names across the class,
Of what they mean - I'd rather not ask!

Immaturity comes to mind
When you find a sticker put on from behind,
Saying 'kick me' or 'push me down'
But all girls do is tut or frown.

We're not as silly as boys, you see,
Who have to get you back,
They'd make it their life's destiny to make
Your eyes black.

But they can be really sweet,
When they're fully grown.
So don't worry girls,
They'll change on their own!

Kathryn McCandless (11)

GIRLS DIFFER FROM BOYS

The story begins when we were small,
Boys are smelly snails, best friend and all.
Boys act like little stupid fools,
Whilst girls are really posh and cool.
Girls are with pretty curls,
Boys are with vicious swells.
Because girls are mature,
Whilst boys are immature.
Girls are daddies' angels,
Boys are mummies' animals.

Boys are now men,
Girls are now women.
Will their feelings stay the same?
Or will it go on and on like a game?

Fateha Begum (13)

IT'S NOT TOO LATE

Leaves of green, leaves of gold,
Falling to the ground so cold,
Spring, summer, winter and the fall,
I have been there, done it and seen it all,
The sun, the sea and the sand,
This is our planet and our precious land,
Save what we have got before it's too late,
There will be nothing left so close the gate,
Stop the destruction and save what we have got,
Oil spillage, pollution and animals being shot,
We must act now before we realise,
The ozone layer has grown to an enormous size,
There will be nothing left for anyone to see,
So please stop this madness and let everything be free.

Sandy Grebby

COMING OF AGE

You are leaving your home
In search of adventure
Another land - another world.
But all is not perfect out there
Different 'ways' - different cultures
Where will you sleep?
What will you eat?
All alone on a 'different street'
You say you know best
On this 'first time' abroad
Travelling through different countries and such
No doubt sleeping rough
But remember your home-land
Whenever you can
We can't stop you going
Now you're a man
So, God go with you Son,
As you 'chance to roam'
Then 'if be', come safely home.

Margaret Parnell

ANDREA JENNET (1986)

Sometimes, when the night is lonely,
I sit and watch you as you sleep.
I listen to your even breathing.
This vigil is so sweet to keep.
The rain can fall against the window,
Yet still I sit beside the bed.
The moonlight casts its silver shadows,
They bounce and dance around your head.
Your hair, a golden cloud of moonbeams;
Your eyelashes flutter on your cheek.
I rise to leave, then bend to kiss you.
I turn, but at the door I peek.
Little child I feel so humble.
I watch your chest, each rise and fall.
Your baby voice is soft and gentle,
Yet I hear you every time you call.
Again I stand framed in the doorway.
I cannot bear to leave you there,
So I sit back down, and watch you sleeping
In the chilly, silent, midnight air.

Jan Lingard

THE PAUSE OF PEACE

A wicked man stands still
While a peaceful man fits the bill

Mr Blair don't be too hasty
'Cos war isn't tasty

Leave it to the few
Those who have more than just a clue

Damage done blocks out the sun
Because of weapons more powerful than a gun

Let's not get involved
Because killings never solved

They just create bad feeling
With the lives they are stealing

It could get out of hand
And destroy all the land

Crops will no longer grow
There may as well be layers of snow
With a mushroom cloud aglow
So bury the past and do it fast
Unleash world peace so the fightings cease
Before there's an unperishable pause of peace . . .
Pitch-black peace
Black peace forever.

Tay Collicutt

Shadows Calling

Death did rest upon my arm, after gentle changing from eagle to raven I befriended the Reaper in darkened feathered appearance. I know not why but at ease was I with this raven perched upon my arm and the raven not the least bit show of alarm.

The reason for our fellowship I cannot recall but together we shall stand tall.

The legend of death in a raven's form did rest upon my arm and at my calling we were as one. To find my feet I stretch from my crouch and with me Shadow does follow. Like the Angel of Death contrary this curse is moreover a guardian angel.

Alliance with that of this angel gives confidence in my predictions, insight into the future sees my path clear. Where does this calling of Shadow come from?

Dragon

ALUN ARMSTRONG!
(Middlesbrough Football Player)

Alun Armstrong, watch his skill,
watch out players, he's out to kill.
Fans and supporters love him so,
in the goal the ball does go.
So much style and so much class,
absolutely fantastic pass!
Plays football ever so brill,
never stops to sit 'n' chill!
Good defender but excellent striker,
absolutely smacks the 'Mitre'.
So happy and bubbly, fair and kind,
makes sure all autographs are fully signed.
So many goals for one football team,
I'm beginning to wonder if you're just a dream.
To round this off in a basic way,
Alun you're great, in every way.

Kimberley M Rushforth

A WORLD FOR THE FUTURE . . .

Every day now, you will see,
Newspaper articles with 'It's the end of the world!' and
'When will it be?'
The simple answer is not for another million years,
So why are we all breaking out in tears?

The colourful environment is getting a little scruff,
And the nature all around us is finding it very tough,
To defend their family and homes because there are so many hunters about,
Even under water, loads of fish are being caught such as salmon and sea trout.

A beer can and sweet wrappers dropped on the floor,
A cigarette, a crisp packet, an old apple core,
A tissue, a plastic cup, a piece of bubble-gum,
A shopping bag, a cardboard box and a half-eaten plum . . .

And what about the smoking and pollution in the air,
People keep on damaging their health but they don't even care!

That's all I can say, so let's call it a day,
Opps! Just one more thing,
To everyone who is yawning,
Listen to my poem, or it may be the last,
If we all don't do something very, *very* fast!

Kerrie Nightingale

Your Arms About Me

I feel your arms about me,
  Your fingers touching my fingertips,
   Your hair brushing my face,
    Cheek against cheek,
     And eyes that tell me
      All I want to know.

Knowing you hold me
 Lying as we do
  Within each other's arms
   Because we care enough
    To be a single term,
     Not two but one.

No words, just love,
 And laughter and warmth,
  And moving this way together.
   With no guilt or jealousy
    Me needing you, you needing me
     And feeling your arms about me.

Joan E Blissett

FIELDS OF ADVENTURE

The grass was long and brambly
in the field at the back of our house.
I remember the old cock-chafer -
and maybe a few field mice.
But that did not deter us,
excitement would beckon us young,
to wander through secret twinding lanes
and oh! We'd have such fun.
We'd camp beneath the bushes
betwixt the bluebell wood,
playing around for many hours
until it was time for bed.

Sometimes we played in another field
where many butterflies flew.
With cow-pats, thistles and dandelion clocks,
and the brightest of buttercups grew.
The cricket field was inviting.
They'd built a brand new hut.
We couldn't find the key,
but my sister would clamber up,
peering in the window to see what she could see,
a treasure-trove of biscuits!
She'd offer one to me.
Sometimes she'd climb an apple tree,
but no - I wouldn't dare.
What if the farmer should catch us
but she didn't seem to care.
Everything has changed most of the fields are gone -
but I'll always remember the happy times
when we had lots of fun.

Wendy Watkin

Autumn

As autumn nights begin to freeze
The cool green garments of the trees
Are changed to brown and red and gold
And as more icy and more cold
The autumn winds begin to blow
The leaves fall to the ground below
To spread an apron on earth's lap
Beneath which soil and seeds and bulbs
Can take their winter's nap
To wake again, refreshed, revived,
When winter's gone and springtime has arrived.

__Dan Pugh__